Balancing Act

How God Wants You to Prioritize Your Life

Advantage™
INSPIRATIONAL

Pat Brochu

I dedicate this book to Heidi, my lovely wife. Without her this book would not have happened. And Kurtis...dad loves you.

Pat Brochu

Acknowledgements

There are several people I must thank:

To Mr. Jack Armaly, who helped me out a great deal with the book.

To my brother-in-law, Mark Sweeney for all of the technical support that was needed.

To the Leadership at our home church, who not only teach the Word, but walk it out daily and are there to encourage you to press into what the Lord has for you. For all of that, Pastor Gerrie and Pastor Claude, thank you.

And last, but not least, to mom and dad, who made a difficult decision several years ago. They did it knowing there would be a price, and still went forward. Thanks , mom and dad.

Pat Brochu

Table of Contents

Pat Brochu

Foreword

This account of Pat Brochu's sexual struggles and despair in his early years is one of the most honest and revealing stories I have ever read.

Because I am the pastor of the church that Pat now attends and have seen the growth that has taken place not only in his character but in the confidence that he now displays, I am honored to present this foreword to his book "The Balancing Act".

Pat is one of those men who literally now lives the teaching of this church and the Word of God, and deserves the credit for lighting a candle rather than cursing the darkness.

His book is one where his openness and candor allows him to speak in the first person about a topic which men find difficult to discuss because of fear and pride. It is easy reading because he speaks from his heart. Most men will relate to the difficulties he faced and be able to see that success comes from a true intimate relationship with Jesus Christ.

There are certain principles running through the book. Humility is one of them. Pat displays humility by not trying to justify himself. He shows that we need compassion, not pity. His book shows the power of God's love.

I recommend this book to anyone who is facing this same battle. As the Lord set Pat free, He will do the same for each one who comes to Him. May the reading of this book affect you profoundly.

Gerrie Armaly
Senior Pastor and Founder
Antioch Christian Ministries Inc.

Chapter One

TIRED OF CHURCH?

This is one of those chapters that you really don't know how to start. Thinking about it, the best way to start is from the beginning- just so I don't miss anything.

We were never a really religious family. We were Catholics.

That's what my grandparents were, my parents were, and I was too...I guess? We would attend mass on Easter and Christmas Eve, and that was about all. I was also attending Catholic School-just two doors down from the church. I had my first Communion, and I followed all of the other traditions as well- Ash Wednesday and going to Confession every couple of months. Going in, you would tell the priest everything wrong you had done. He would tell you to say several Hail Mary's and Our Father's, and you would walk out of there feeling good about yourself.

The fact is, at a young age, I had horrible language. I remember going to church with my cousins and aunt once, but I had forgotten all about this. The only thing I did remember was looking up at a woman whose mouth was wide open. My cousin squeezed my neck very hard, and took me out of church. My aunt told me immediately that she would never take me to church again-and she didn't. You may ask, "You remember all of that, but you can't recall what you said?" No! This is because I didn't think what I had said was wrong. Years later, we all had a good laugh when my cousin brought it up, and told me what had happened.

He told me that we were both going up for Communion. I hadn't had my first Communion yet, but I did everything my cousin did; walk in that wedding rhythm with my hands out in front of me. I got up there, and NOTHING! The priest gave a host to him, and not me. So I said, "Eh, the !#@?ER didn't give me one!" I learned very quickly that that was a BAD word, and being in a church didn't help.

As an adult, when I would meet up with people from my past, that's all I would hear; "I remember when you were a kid; you swore like a sailor!" At this time, it was embarrassing.

I remember going to my aunt's retirement party. Sitting at the table, I recognized the man next to me. I said, "Hey, Mr. So and So (I'll leave his name out, as he is still very local); you may not remember me (the last time I saw him I was about 6 or 7, now being 27)". I just wasn't sure if he would remember me. He said, "Oh, I recognize you. You would come out of your aunt's house to my garden, and curse me out". Once again, I had no recollection.

I did remember that I would walk towards him while he was in his garden, and he would always get up and go into the house. I just thought it was bad timing on my part. I looked at him and said, "Good news; I'm older, and I don't swear anymore". I laughed- he didn't. He looked right at me and said, "No, you swore a lot (I remember thinking, this is going to be a great night)!" I looked right at him, and said, "You know what, I'm sorry for that". Even though we were sitting right next to each other, he never said a word to me the entire night.

It was very awkward, but the reason I share this with you is because when I started going to Confession a few years later, something started to take place. Even at a young age, I thought that when I confessed to the priest, it felt good; it seemed like I was starting fresh. And also at a young age, I was starting to put two –and – two together, thinking, good people go to church, and bad people don't. As I got older, I volunteered to be an alter boy; just to step it up a notch. I felt better than my classmates, and even though I didn't realize it, that is where religion started for me. The funny thing is, I still kept swearing and fighting in school, but when I'd go get that little spiritual tune-up, I was back on track.

Things started to change in our lives as a family. We had moved down from Quebec a year earlier. However, before we moved down, I saw my dad going hunting with one of my uncle's rifles. Mom was washing dishes, so I asked if I could go along with him (dad never went hunting). My mom firmly said "NO".

What I didn't realize was that dad was actually going in the back woods to kill himself. When dad came back, he had shot himself a couple of rabbits. I didn't think much of it. Years later, dad told me that that is when he accepted the Lord-that day he went hunting. The Lord changed his life drastically! I could see it-dad was happier. We have pictures of dad before and after, and the difference was like night and day!

After this, we moved back to Ontario, and started to attend church more often; like every Sunday! We went to a small little church with about 200 people or so. The first time we walked into that church- I was about 8- people started clapping their hands and thanking God. We had relatives that attended the church, and they had the whole church- and I mean the WHOLE church- praying for us. I thought that was the strangest thing! That was where we attended church for many years, but I was still a troublemaker (I always seemed to hang out with the other troublemakers). If anything was broken at church, dad knew I was involved in some way, but then something happened.

On December 31, 1983, at ten years old, I gave my heart to the Lord. Did I fully know what I had done? No! However, I did know that I was going to heaven. That was about as deep as it got for me. We attended church very regularly. If you weren't sick and stayed home, you stayed in your bedroom the whole time with no games or toys, so it was better to go to church.

My little attitude of: "I'm better than you because I never miss church" was always there, but never spoken of. Years later, that's what it was all about; just going to church, sitting in the back right hand corner, and always wearing nice, expensive clothing.

My thing was wearing cool ties (with old T.V. show characters on them: I Love Lucy, The Three Stooges, Little Rascals, etc.).They were expensive. Like everyone else, for me it was about status, until one day dad asked me a question.

I was about 22, still living at home, and looking through the auto trader; checking out the price of 'Vettes'. I was thinking about maybe picking one up in the spring. I remember Dad saying, "If you died tonight, would you make it to Heaven?" I think everyone has had that question asked of them at least once in their life, but I couldn't give that knee-jerk reaction of: "Oh, yes, I'm going to heaven".

I got very angry at God because I thought He didn't think I was good enough. I gave Him my tithe and went to church twice on Sundays. I always wore nice clothing. My mustang was parked across the street, and it was always spotless- I mean always spotless (I even cleaned the motor by hand). I listened to mom and dad, worked very hard, and I didn't drink, smoke, or do drugs. Yet…I doubted that God was going to let me into Heaven. My attitude was: "Well, if that's the way You want to play, then You stay on Your side, and I'll stay on mine". This went on for years; going to church, smiling and trying to be a decent guy.

Working with the men's ministry at our church now, I see something different about myself; I liked going to church, but I didn't like God. That was strange, because for most of the guys it seemed to be the opposite; they didn't mind God, but just didn't like church. That showed me that God will meet us wherever we are.

Several years later, something happened that really shocked my world. Mom mentioned that they were looking at switching churches. That was a J.F.K. moment. I was in my sister's apartment. Mark (my brother-in-law) was on afternoons, and mom was going into the kitchen. I thought, oh, mom's just saying that. We had been at that church for 19 years. We were never really allowed to talk about the church; Dad would always say, "Oh, pray about it", or, "Just pray for the pastor and for our leadership". Mom and dad were involved with the church, and everything seemed o.k. To hear this news -just like that- was shocking.

I can remember calling dad from my truck phone the next day. He said, "Yes, we are looking at leaving, but I'll talk about it with you tonight". When I hung up the phone, reality hit me. Was it true? This was immediately followed with thoughts of all the Hell it was going to bring with it.

It was simple. When you left the church, you left with the clothes on your back, and that was about it. Your name was on a fresh roll of toilet paper. In the church, it was just that simple. It's just like in the movie, The Godfather, when Michael says to Fredo; "I love you, but don't ever go against the family again".

The reason I knew this was because it wasn't the first time several families had left all at once. We would just sit in our seats at the church and look at how good we were for not leaving, like "those people". I knew the way the chef served them up, and I realized that it was going to happen again, only this time the ingredients were going to be my family. It wasn't fun.

I remember talking to dad the night before he was going to talk to the pastor. He was sitting on the edge of his bed, setting the alarm clock for work, when I told him, "Do you realize that the decision you're making is not just going to affect you, but your children and your grandchildren, as well?" Dad answered back, choking up a little; "I've never been so scared in my life; it was easier to quit a job of 18 years with a pension than to make this decision". The reason why I mentioned that to dad was because I was nervous and I didn't know if he was off or right on target.

Months later, I saw it for myself. Dad was right on the money, and I left. When you left, you left all of your friends behind. It was challenging, and a little painful, but more upsetting.

Once again, I was upset at God for allowing this to happen, so I really didn't like talking to Him much. If I would hear anything from God, it would always sound like He was upset with me.

The Lord showed me later; the reason why He was always correcting me was because I always thought I was better than everyone else. I would point at them with my little crooked Christian finger and pass judgment on them when their issues were none of my business.

The Lord put it to me this way-He used my son, Kurtis, as an example. He said, "You want to have fun with him later when he gets older, right? You could teach him to use a remote-control car, boat, or plane. You're looking forward to having fun with him, but if Kurtis chooses to rebel, criticize and give you a hard time, then all the fun things you wanted to do with him will be put on hold until all of these issues are dealt with".

At the time, I didn't realize that I had a bad attitude, and I thought that God was a big thug- that He was out to make me miserable. It really took years for me to see that we serve a great and patient God. I started to attend another church, and boy! You remember the first church-where they were clapping on the way in? That was nothing compared to this church!

Dad had told me that this church was a little bit more alive. Boy, was that an understatement! The first time I came, there was a guy laughing behind me the whole time-not loud, but you could hear the hissing sound a smoker makes when he laughs. Well, that was it! I can remember looking at dad, and he was looking right back at me, laughing! I thought, "It's too much!" In the past, if you clapped too loud, you were getting "the look" from people, but what I saw here was that the people were really worshipping God.

I left with something I didn't know existed in churches-HOPE, and I started to attend regularly.

A couple of months later, I started dating my beautiful wife, Heidi (now of 7 years). I never wanted much of God- just to kind of be on His good side. I can remember saying many times; "Well, if I make it to Heaven by the skin of my teeth, that's fine with me!"

There was something in me that wanted more, but I just didn't know how to get there. This also went on for years- sitting in the back row. My excuse was, I'm a big guy, so out of respect for others, I'll sit back here. At the time, we had a small sanctuary, but really- I just didn't want to get involved or bother.

Sometimes (with some songs), there would be dancing involved, and people would try to get me to move and dance. I would just laugh and think, move away from me, nutcase. At 400 lbs, they would have had to get a couple of ushers involved-just kidding! Even though I had changed churches and was under different leadership, my problems were still there. I would hear our Head Pastor say, "The Lord's presence is here". Some people would pray, and some of them were at the altar. I would look at the clock and think, this is definitely going into extra innings!

I would get upset at God that, once again, He would pick a few people that He would bless and let them feel His presence, but not me. It brought that anger all back up again, reminding me of when dad asked me if I was going to Heaven, and I didn't "feel" like I was. Everything was stirring up again. I would pray – nothing. I would pray for something- and nothing happened. It just felt like God could care less about me. Everyone looked like their lives were in order. They looked happy-and I put on that smile, too; but deep down inside,

I was "ticked off" that no one cared, and God didn't care either.

The only thing I loved about church was that it was about 12 minutes away at 100mph.The pickup was governed, and I could crank the music loud! I love car audio with the window open! You couldn't hear the wind at that speed- now that was nice and loud!

But then you were right back in the back row watching the clock again. As soon as it was over, I would say bye to dad and jump in the truck (at the time, Heidi was working at a nursing home on the weekends).

But there was nothing for me there. The church is and was alive, but it would go right past me. I would ask myself, "Why do I keep going?" It was simple. When I was a 9 year old kid; "good people went to church, and bad people didn't". I know it doesn't make any sense, but that's where I was.

I was just getting more and more frustrated at God, and Heidi was without a doubt the spiritual head of the home. I felt that God liked to listen to Heidi much better than to me. This went on for 2 years. Heidi asked me a question once and said, "If you were on your deathbed (or something to that effect), what would be your biggest regret in life?"

I told her that my biggest regret in life would be not ever competing in a world championship high-end car audio competition with a very expensive car. Heidi said, "Well, let's do it!" Within 6 months, I had looked at a lot of high-end SUV's, but the one that felt right was the Cadillac Escalade. I was 31 at the time, so I thought it would make me happy. It did for the first month and then I realized that there were 71 more months of basically having a second mortgage. Heidi and I started to buy and order a lot of expensive equipment for the stereo I was building-which took close to a year and $13,000.00- no joke!

Heidi saw that I was working long hours, and surprised me one day by saying, "I'm paying for your whole weekend to go to the world championship car audio competition". It was being held in Louisville, Kentucky that year, and I asked Heidi to go with me – just to truly show her why I loved it so much! There's just something about 165dbs that moves your jeans at about 50 feet away! It just makes you smile!

This was where the big guns were-all of the guys I spent hours and hours reading about just to get ideas from them! And there he was; the world champion. This was a guy that came in after his car was polished, and his stereo balanced. This was the guy! In all the car magazine pictures, he always had the biggest smile- like he knew he had a great life! He worked with one of the industry's biggest names, and was known all over the world as the Grand Master of car audio. Heidi told me to go talk to him, but I didn't want to. He was sitting on a big Tupperware container, and he looked... well, he looked disappointed. That hit me hard, because that was what I was aiming for, and I looked happier than him!

So I went and shook his hand and told him I loved his car and his great work in sound. I asked him what a rookie like me should expect, and he started to tell me that there were a lot of politics involved. He told me that you didn't want to get on the bad side of any of the judges. Needless to say, I walked away not just ticked off, but disappointed. I was upset at Heidi for making me go and talk to him, believe it or not. I was quickly starting to see and realize that the answers to happiness weren't there.

I felt trapped. I was going to church, didn't feel God, and I couldn't get joy out of the world, either. I was really starting to build up anger towards God. Now I see (I couldn't at the time because of the anger) that the Lord was starting to work on my heart. He was giving me the chance to get all the toys I wanted, but it wasn't filling the hole inside of me. Things were starting to change quickly!

Chapter Two

LIFE IN THE BACK ROW

I never listened to Christian radio music because I thought Christian music was terrible. There were three Christian artists, and I didn't care for them much. Listening to a secular channel one day, the song started and it hit me right in the chest. I can remember thinking, this is a great song, and it almost sounded like a Christian song!

The artist was Switchfoot, and the words were "This is your life, are you who you want to be?" and "This is your life like is it everything that you dreamed that it would be?"

The answer for me was a big .NO! It was cool that my friend, Vaughn had made me a mixed CD. I kept pressing repeat over and over listening to these words.

I was asked to be an usher, so I started doing that. My thought was, if I get involved with something, I'll feel more a part of things". However, that went away very fast, as sometimes you had to usher at the early service; you had to be there for 7:30 a.m. on a Sunday. You didn't feel closer to God; if anything (if your heart wasn't right), you would think He was laughing at you. I always had negative thoughts towards God, and it was hard talking to anyone about it. As a man, you didn't want anyone to know that this was bothering you, or was even a big deal to you, but it was. This went on for months. It didn't need to, but pride will always get in the way. Then something started to happen.

I was starting to get bummed out big time, so I went to visit my dad. He warned me, "It's one thing to be bummed out, but don't get involved with depression". He asked me what I would dwell on all day, and what kind of music I listened to. I didn't realize that half of my CD's in the truck were Country music (don't get me wrong- if you like that it's up to you, but for me, it was all those sad songs-and all that came with it).I didn't even like Country music much. The Lord really had His work cut out for Him.

I told the Lord one time that there was nothing on earth more depressing than to see a guy at the bar getting drunk by himself (as you can see, I was paying more attention to Country music than I thought).The Lord responded with, "There is actually something even worse. It's a man that goes to church week after week after week with no friends and no relationships with anyone". That's the worst, because if the body of Christ isn't there for him, then what else is out there for him?

I could remember we, as a family, would go to Florida every 2 years. I always had my trusted little perverted jokes. When we were at Sea World watching the whales jumping around and doing tricks, I looked down, and there it was. There was a girl sitting in front of my seat, and you could see a tattoo on her lower back. She was also wearing a thong-Man, now that was a show! I would look down here and there; not making it too obvious. I had my camcorder along, and I was going to videotape it as a joke-right in the middle of our family video. I didn't, and I am very glad now, because it would have ruined the tape for everyone.

Right there on the spot, I began to feel a conviction that I had never really had before. Looking at girls in the past, I would give them a once-over in church or on the street, and never really feel bad. Normally, this was a treat or a bonus for me, but it frustrated me that I could look without feeling wrong, but I was going to church, and feeling conviction. I felt stuck.

Several months before this, I had started to get upset at the leadership in our church. They would never talk to me; sometimes they would walk around me and keep going. This just added to my belief that the whole church was there to take care of the first 3 rows; Pastors, Elders, Deacons, etc…I felt like a nobody- just there to open the door for them. I was starting to see the same behavior as at the old church.

Talking to dad(I would always wear a baseball cap because when I got upset and started to sweat, I would lose focus with having to wipe down my forehead), I shared with him all of the problems I saw in leadership. He said, "You're seeing too much. You need to do one of two things: either stay and go talk to the Pastor, or get out of the church". I went home to plead my case to Heidi (of course I was upset; with sweat running down my back), and I was yelling and swearing. Heidi replied, "So that's it; you're not going to church anymore?"

I really didn't know what to do, but there was still something there. I couldn't explain it, but that night (or morning), I went to bed at 5:00 a.m., slept in on Sunday, and just didn't care. Even still, the Lord was starting to speak to me at some of the oddest times.

I was reading my car audio magazine as usual, and at the time, one of the guys in there had 244 trophies-some of them over 7 feet tall. He was old school-everything was balanced by measuring and installing speakers. That is a very hard job, but this guy was in the expert category. Reading through, I was just looking for audio clues. I thought, I would love to have a huge trophy downstairs in the pool room, and to start having the reputation of being one of the World's best- and all the stories that would go with it. The Lord spoke to me right there in my room and said, "Yes, it would be a great thing to have those trophies, but then what? Look at all the trophies he's proud of his children may put 2 or 3 of them in their homes out of respect, but his grandchildren may only have one, and a couple of stories to tell. If you give me your all, I will do something your great, great grandchildren will know of, and you will have a great heritage".

That was great, but also confusing because I was seriously starting to think about switching churches and Heidi and I were basically on the same page. Then I heard the Lord say again, "Do this for me; talk to your pastor, and ask all of the questions you want to. Tell her all of the problems you are seeing". He basically told me to empty out my whole bucket and leave nothing behind.

Well, I thought pastors were always so busy-it seemed like that's what I would always hear. It could take months to get to talk to her- but I was willing to wait. When I approached Pastor Gerrie, I said, "I don't usually make appointments like this, but I would like to ask you some questions".

I warned her that it could take a while, so I would bring pizza, water and a sleeping bag. She laughed and said, "I have an opening on Tuesday". My quick reply was, "of this month?"

That really struck me. I started to wonder- who put the thought in my head that it would take a month? When the day of the appointment came, I went into the office expecting to ask a couple of good questions, and then be asked to leave. This is because in the past (not at this church), under the same circumstances you would have been asked to leave, and not to come back. This time, however, something different happened.

Pastor Gerrie started answering all of my questions honestly! I could see that she was sincere. I then asked her a more personal question- and it wasn't a very big question- but she looked right at me, and said, "You're right; that is an area that the Lord needs to help me with". Just like that, I was confused. It was like watching the T.V. show COPS (when they do that pit maneuver; the police hit the back corner of your car, putting you into a tailspin). This definitely put me into a tailspin! My way of thinking had always been that pastors were perfect, and priests were perfect- that they were the closest thing to Heaven on earth. In the past, it seemed to be the way it was, because that was what the pastor wanted. I thought of them as intermediaries- we went through them to speak to God.

Next, Pastor Gerrie asked me a question; "When was the last time you read your Bible?" My thought was, I'm looking at the door anyways, so I told her, "Over 3 years ago. The Bible is one of the most boring books I've looked through". I would always fall asleep reading it.

After speaking with Pastor Gerrie for a couple of hours, she asked if it would be alright to pray with me. I agreed, and she started. Oh boy! Suddenly the back of my head got really hot (blow-dryer hot)! It didn't make any sense. I'm a big guy; I'm usually hot, but not that hot! My eyes were closed, and I started to see something.

It felt like that feeling you get when you push your thumbs too hard into your eyes- only I wasn't! Then I saw it. I seemed to be standing in the middle of smoke going up on either side of me with pressure. It was grey all around me, and I was looking straight up. A patch of clear blue sky about the size of my fist was starting to open up directly above me. It would contract- bigger, then smaller. I heard a voice say, "I will start revealing myself to you much clearer".

Right after this vision, Pastor Gerrie said exactly the same thing! This really freaked me out! She then prayed, "Lord, please cause the Bible to start coming alive to him. Amen". So, I thanked her (let me just clarify- I was always respectful towards her because she was, after all, my pastor), and left the office.

Driving home, I had a massive headache, and I never have headaches. I was so confused; I had seriously been thinking of leaving the church, but if I had a Pastor who was that honest, did I really want to leave? Talking out loud in the SUV, I was not at all respectful towards God when I said, "I don't know what the HELL You want, but I have nothing to offer You". It got very quiet in the SUV, and all I heard Him say was, "That's all I needed to hear".

I wasn't sure if God had left me...or what? The next day, I went to work as usual. Sitting at the Ambassador Bridge at 5:00 a.m., I remembered that I had a Bible in the back of my truck. Pastor Gerrie had prayed and asked God to make the Bible come alive to me, so I thought I would give it a try. I started in Matthew, and immediately I could picture the story in my head!

I began to see the reason I was always mad at God. I felt as if I had always put my very best forward (clean car, nice clothing, always smiling, and being a good person). All of these nice things were laid out on a display table. The Lord would walk by, say "No, not good enough", and keep on walking. This wasn't at all the case; the Lord hadn't asked me to do all of those things. He just wanted ME, period!

One of the first things the Lord asked me to work on was my thought life. When I would drive the truck in the city, I had to pay attention, but when I would drive on the highway, I didn't have to focus nearly as much.

My thoughts would wander around, and here's a warning: when the Lord asks you to work on something- heads up! You will get attacked with the opposite! Case in point; when the Lord asked me to work on my thought life, I thought it would change- you know; fuzzy bunnies, sunsets- that sort of thing. What really happened was completely different.

I was going to pay my toll on the U.S. border. When I saw the truck in front of me starting to pull ahead, I started to follow about 2 feet behind him so that I would get to the booth faster.

The woman in charge of the toll booth was already shaking her head like she was saying, "no", so I quickly put the truck into reverse. There was no one behind me, so I thought she was closing. However, she motioned for me to come up. When I got to the booth, she was already yelling at me! I didn't have any idea of who she was. I hadn't seen her in the past, or ever spoken to her before, yet here she was yelling, "I told you yesterday not to pull up on the scale, but to wait your turn!"

It was 5:00 in the morning, and I was not in the mood to get yelled at by a "cash box operator". I wanted to swipe the card, and tell her to "shut it, thank you", but the Lord was telling me to be nice to her. So, I asked her if she may have mistaken me for someone else, but she said, "No, I talked to you". Now at the border, there are over 11,000 trucks that clear every day, so she did get me mixed up with someone else. When she kept going on and on, I asked her for my card back, and left.

This is where I battled- going down the highway. It started with my thoughts; did you see the size of her; she made you look small. The Lord would always say, "No, don't give in to that- stop thinking of her that way". I would stop, but 2 minutes later the thoughts would come; looks like she was smoking, too. She probably has 14 cats at home. My pants would be too small for her! I would stop thinking of her that way, but 2 minutes later, there were more thoughts; She probably drives a 1984 minivan, all rusted out, with the material hanging down from the ceiling!

Once again, I said, "No, I will not think of her that way!" When I said it this time, the big knot in my stomach was gone! It had taken a total of approximately 15 minutes, but afterwards it didn't bother me for the rest of the day!

The next morning, I thought, O.k., she was at that booth yesterday, so I shot all of the way across (about 10 booths over). Just like that, there she was again! Once again, the truck ahead of me was pulling away. I had the thought of pulling up just to shove it in her face, but the Lord said, "No, don't!" He also told me to say, "Good morning" to her, so I did. She smiled, like this was her first time meeting me!

Believe it or not, this happened 5 days in a row! Every day, I would go to a different booth to avoid her, and every day she would be there! The Lord was showing me my heart- my thoughts were a handful and needed a lot of work. Slowly, my attitude started to change; not overnight, but daily. I was starting to talk to the Lord more, but I didn't really trust Him. My way of thinking was, I will have to give Him my all, and I didn't want to lose any of my stuff (the house, my 'Caddy', or my toys). Once again, it was the enemy who was putting those thoughts in my head!

After I realized that it wasn't God, but the enemy sending those negative thoughts, I was able to start pushing those thoughts away (with God's help)!

Ushering at church one Sunday morning, I saw a Promise Keeper's flyer. I didn't know they still existed – I had gone to one at the Pontiac Silver Dome about 10 years earlier! At the time, there had been over 72,000 men there- which freaks you out, because that is a lot of people! When I saw the flyer, I heard God say, "I need you to be there", so I went- along with several other men from the church. Although it was clear the Lord wanted me to be there, I still didn't know why.

When the first speaker at Promise Keepers came out, he had long hair and a goatee! He looked like Val Kilmore, but shorter and stockier. This man would go to local Universities and debate religion. He started off by saying, "When you go to debate, they try to intimidate you by saying, 'I hate religion with a passion!' He would respond with, "I hate religion also!" Now here I was at a PK event, and the guest speaker just said he hated God?! I really thought he was going to be escorted out- we were in a church for crying out loud! Then he said, "So let's talk about Jesus". That really confused me, because I always thought that Jesus was the beginning of religion. He spoke for 40 minutes about the difference between "religion" and "Jesus".

That was my divine appointment- that was why I was there. I had a lump in my throat the size of a basketball and my eyes were watering up, but I didn't- did not let anyone know (I was with men from church).

Afterwards, I went and purchased his book, <u>The End of Religion </u>(it's a great book). As I shook his hand, I told him, "I've been in church for over 24 years now, and it's finally making sense tonight". He saw that I was having a hard time finishing my sentence, so all he said was, "I know, man, I know".

What I saw that night was the veil of religion lifted; I saw Jesus clearly. I remember the Lord saying, "You and I are much closer than you think". The thing I had hated all my life wasn't God- it was all the rules to get to God- and there were no rules. When Jesus died on the cross 2000 years ago, it was so that we could have access to Him by ourselves. Don't get me wrong- we still need our pastors there to help us, but I could go to Him anywhere!! I hated kneeling by my bed and closing my eyes- now I talk to him all the time in my truck!

There were still some hard tasks, but it was getting easier. I was finally really starting to understand what that man was talking about; everyone's religion started out with good intentions, reverencing and trusting God, but they quit having fellowship with God, and started focusing more on their traditions. Every generation would do something more and more reverential than their parents and grandparents.

Now no one can get near God because of everything they need to do for Him. He never asked us to do those things, but out of respect to our families, that's the way we did it. You felt like you couldn't talk to God yourself. Because the priest (or pastor) had his life in order, he was better able to communicate with God than you were. These were all lies. It's true that priests and pastors must have their lives in order, but God can and will meet you wherever you are. He is still able to speak directly to you.

I once heard a pastor (and I use that term very loosely because it insults the real pastors out there) say, "Many of you believe that you hear from God. Tell me what He said, and I will tell you if that was the Lord or not". That is flat out religion and job security!! If you have a hard time deciding if it is the Lord or not, that's when you approach the pastor, but don't ever let a pastor look down on you for not understanding. If their heart is right, they will encourage you to keep on listening. The reason I can say that is because I am blessed with a great team of pastors that always encourage me to keep pressing into the Lord.

Even though the Lord was starting to come alive to me, I still didn't feel as though I wanted to "give Him my all". I was definitely seeing God differently, though.

One day, I was driving on 96 West just out of Detroit near Newburg Road, when the Lord asked me, "What do you think of Me?" In my thoughts I said, "Do You want me to be honest, or do You want me to tell You what You want to hear?" I heard Him say, "No, be honest". I grabbed the steering wheel tightly with both hands, and said, "I think You're mean, controlling and manipulative". I'm not joking- everything in the truck went silent. After a pause, all I heard was, "Why?"

I said, "Why? Why do I think of You like that; because…?" I had nothing- no reason to think of Him that way. God followed up with, "When you close your eyes and think of Me, what do you see?" That was easy- I can describe the impression to you clearly. There were black marble floors; flawless like a mirror, a 20-foot ceiling (like in a palace), and very big pillars with a golden chair. This chair was decorated like a king's chair would be (with cranberry velour). Jesus was sitting on the chair with a royal robe on, and He was wearing a little rope around His waist (like a tassel you would use to hold curtains back). He was sitting there with a very large staff- not talking to us, but tapping the floor with it to get our attention, and moving His head in every direction. He wanted us to go in, but He was not communicating with us.

Once again, the Lord asked me "Why?" I didn't have an answer as to why I saw Him that way. I could only come up with one reply; "Well, that's how we were treated by one of Your little puppets down here". The Lord said, "I had nothing to do with that; that is not how I am". So, I asked the Lord, "How are you?" Right there, going down the highway, I had a vision.

I was standing in a hole that was the beginning of a new house. This hole was roughly 50 feet by 60 feet and about 4 feet deep. It was muddy, and I saw the exact same person that had been sitting on the royal throne. He was now working with a sledge hammer, knocking out the footing of a foundation. This person was working very hard, and I could hear every grunt before each hit he made to destroy the footing. I asked him, "Why are you doing this for me?"

As he stopped and looked up, I saw that it was Jesus. Sweating, and covered in mud, He answered, "…because I love you. Up until now, I wasn't sure how far I had to go with you, but now I know. We're going to start fresh from the bottom, and hang on- it won't take long". He went willingly back to work then.

Just like that, I was back in the truck. The vision only took a few seconds (It took longer to write it out), but it impacted me deeply.

I felt so much joy for days afterwards! One night something happened. I was pulling into a truck stop (not exactly the most spiritual place, but the Lord was there big time), and normally I would start fueling up, and jump back in the truck to do some paperwork. This time was different.

It had been a long day beginning at 4:00 a.m. (it was now about 8:00 p.m.), and God suddenly told me to stop everything. When I think about this, it puts a huge knot in my throat. When I tried to explain it once to Pastor Claude, I couldn't finish. Instead, I grabbed a water bottle out of the fridge, and quickly changed the subject. When I heard God say that, I stopped. I leaned up against a yellow safety pole, and looked up at the sky.

The sky was bright blue, and the moon was out. The sun was down, but was still bright on the horizon.

As I took a deep breath, and looked at the moon, I knew that I was at peace with God for the first time in my life. If anything were to happen to me, I knew that I was at peace with my Maker- there was just a peace between God and I. I also knew that the Lord would take care of Heidi for me (Kurtis hadn't been born yet).

I've been asked a few times, "What happened to turn you around so fast?" Like I said a few paragraphs before, once the veil of religion was lifted, I saw Jesus for who He really is. If you ask me what I think of Jesus now; "He's just, He's kind, He's caring, He's merciful, but most of all, He's a good friend. He's there when I'm struggling". So... what do I see when I close my eyes now?

I see a carpenter working in the mud on a new foundation for my life.

Pat Brochu

Chapter Three

THE BIG LIE

As with other parts of this book, I had to begin in prayer: asking the Lord where to begin, and also where the big lie began for me. The Lord once again led me right to it. He showed me that I was the one who had put myself into a rat race that didn't really exist.

I thought that if people were to see me in a big high-end vehicle, they would respect me as a person of success. When I looked at it honestly, I realized that they did not respect me any more or any less. As in previous chapters, this may or may not relate to you. My goal throughout this book is really to get men to just slow down for a minute- or even stop- and look at what is truly important to them. It's like in the movie, City Slickers. Curly is talking to Mitch and tells him that the secret of life is "one thing".

It's up to us to figure out what that one thing is.

We really don't realize or see ourselves as men in a race, but we're always trying to do it better; to let people see how things should be done- and done right! One day you stop, and realize: you fell right into it. Now I don't have statistics or numbers for this, but I hope that as you read, you will be able to relate in some small way.

I can remember when the Lord really started to open my eyes in this area. I was in my early 30's, and so thankful for what God was showing me.

Driving down the highway, I met up with another guy I knew, and began to share with him. I didn't know how old he was, or anything really personal about him, but we had about an hour and a half to kill, so I thought I would share this with him. Now, I don't go into as much detail as I will later, but I just wasn't sure how he was going to take it. I can remember talking to him for about 20 minutes straight on the C.B. I normally didn't do that, because 10 minutes into it he could have taken a phone call, and missed half of the conversation. However, I just couldn't help myself, and talked the whole time! After I finished talking, it was quiet. I remember thinking, oh man, he missed most of it, but he keyed up on the mike, and said, "You just summed up my whole life in 20 minutes- right to a tee". That's when the Lord told me I had to keep notes of this- but enough with the build-up. Let's get to it!

What I shared with him is how (as men) we start off by thinking we are going to show the world how it should be done. This is a shorter version of what I said, but here goes. In your 20's, you are looking to work hard and have fun. In your 30's, you have the mortgage to deal with, and the S.U.V. in the garage. It starts to hit you- if you are going to do something big, now is the time.

You're still young and strong, so you get all the overtime you can. Then in your 40's, you start looking at early retirement, getting that one last big house and putting your kids through College. Once again, you're working overtime. In your early 50's, the kids are gone, the house is big and empty, and you really don't know your wife. Even though the kids are gone, married, or still in school, you're still working hard because that's all there is to do. You start looking, and realize that life passed you right by.

I can remember when I asked the Lord, "Where did it start for me?" He took me back to when I was 15 years old. Dad told me, "If you want anything in life, you have to get off of your *# !@ and go get it- there are no free rides in life!" Dad is and was right, but I quickly took it to the extreme. By age16, I had 3 part-time jobs-and please understand me; I wasn't a workaholic, but it kept me busy, and out of trouble. I worked at Biway stocking the shelves, at a local convenient store, and at my grandfather's lumber yard on the weekends. I can remember- at that age- having all the answers to life, and thinking that I was going to do better than dad (or anyone else out there).

I have very hard-working uncles, and several of them owned a couple of businesses each at the time. I thought that I had to work just as hard to keep up the "family name", and that's exactly what it was- hard work. I can remember buying my 2nd car before I was out of high school. It was a 4 banger Mustang LX, but I really wanted to buy a 5L Mustang before my 21st

birthday. I was working very long and hard hours at the factory. By age 21, I was a supervisor in my shop, and had 7-8 guys that I had trained working under me. Mind you, they didn't speak much English, but eh- I was a supervisor, and that's all that mattered to me!

I can remember when I got the 5L Mustang Cobra GT. I always thought that a young man with a nice car and new shoes was on top of the world- yes, I know; if only it could be that easy! So I got the new car and the new shoes that I was so very proud of. That night, I cruised Ouellette-and took off at a couple of lights a little faster than I should have (that's what the 5L Mustang was for, right?). I remember thinking, "O.k., I did it- now what?" Believe it or not, I had just purchased the car that week-and I was already thinking about what was next.

I need to say this right now; people always say that buying things doesn't make you happy. I'm here to say that it does- it really does. Everyone is happy when they buy stuff, but the question is; for how long? Just like pop, everything- and I mean everything- loses its fizz. Some things lose it faster than others. So there I was thinking, "O.k., it would be nice to have a Corvette at 23 years old", and it started all over again.

I was working at the factory 60-70 hours/week. I would finish at noon on Saturdays. There was just something I loved about being tired, but having had a good work week. There was also a little expensive habit starting up- and no, it wasn't drugs. Everything I owned had to be the best, or I wouldn't touch it. When you're in your early 20's, your car and your clothing are alright, but as you get older, the toys start having more zeros behind them. That's when the real game starts. I would think, "Eh- I'm single and working hard; I deserve all of this stuff!"

I was standing in a storage garage once, looking at the two cars I had (at the time, I had become an owner operator in the trucking business).I was 25 then, and I can remember thinking, I have 2 Mustangs, a pickup, my Semi-truck (which at the time was a show truck), and a very big, very fast snowmobile. At the time it was the biggest- a 900 Triple Thundercat! I thought, I'm making it, and turning heads, but whose heads was I turning? That was a question I had never really sat down and thought about.

I was starting to get into debt pretty fast. Snowmobiling was very expensive in the winter, and in the summer, I had my real love- high-end car audio. Now don't laugh; car audio can get into the tens of thousands of dollars very quickly- but I loved it! I was still looking for happiness, so later on I joined IASCA- International Audio Sound Challenge Association. That's where the big guns played for the world championships. Snowmobiling was also very expensive. It had nothing to do with enjoying the trail; it was about shoving it in that loud-mouthed face at the bar, and being in front on the lake. This is the first time I've said this, but it's been about 10 years now that I've been out of snowmobiling.

What I would do is take the sled out of storage on a Saturday in September, go to the shop, and spend thousands and thousands of dollars. I was still climbing into debt, but I had to be the fastest- and the best. $3,000.00 later, I was one of the fastest! My mechanic told me it was roughly around 180hp (which was sweet when you were running on the lake).When you pulled it out of "storage" in November, it would start with the first pull! One time, a guy pulled up with a 700 Twin Polaris- which was very fast. We were going about 70mph, when he did a 1-2-3-count with his gloves. I stood on the back and pinned it. My front end went up and stayed up until I reached over 100mph! It was a rush, but very, very costly! Sorry, I need to get back on track, because right now I am sweating and wanting to look at getting back into it. What I'm really trying to say is that I could not afford my lifestyle.

At age 27, I met the grandest person in my life- Heidi. We were married 9 months later! It just timed out that way- we were not expecting! I'm very proud to say that nothing happened until after we were married. One day I stopped, looked at it, and said, "How did this happen?" Here I was- in my early 30's, living in the nice big house, with an Escalade in the garage. I was in debt, and looking at working Saturdays to pay the bills.

At the time, I had turned my life back over to the Lord because I was at my wit's end with everything. I had a great life, a great wife, and got along well with my family, but there was still something missing.

The Lord really mapped it out for me. It was so simple, but we all fall into it. We are all searching for happiness, thinking the nice car, the bigger house, or the nice new Semi will do it, but you see that you are still searching. That's where we need to stop for a minute and evaluate our life. Now I know some guys are reading this and thinking, "Oh, he's a quitter", but what are you really quitting? I'm not talking about not paying your bills. What I'm saying is to stop and look at what and why you are doing what you're doing.

I can remember dad telling me about a guy he worked with in the past. He was a workaholic who gave his family everything (a new house, a new car, vacations, etc), but the one thing he forgot about- and that was a very important part of a family- was himself as a father. He realized it too late one day- he came home and the big house was empty. That's normally when we (as men) start looking and evaluating what is really important to us, and maybe it's too late.

The reason I am saying this is not to be ignorant, but because some of you are seeing the warning signs right now, and you have to catch it, or another man will. I don't mean to be a jerk about this, but sometimes we need to hear it or read it to make us stop. I know this is more of an area that the Lord showed me, because I'm not at that age yet. I realize I need to trust the Lord, and I do.

Next, the Lord showed me that you work overtime and budget to get out of debt (which is good) .Then in your early 40's,you begin to work on paying your house off early- so you can get into your "retirement home"(which is that nice $400- $500,000 house). At this time the kids go to College, and you have an extra car payment and tuition. Your wife goes back to work because the kids are all grown up, and you begin to focus on retirement. You probably want to travel, and one day it dawns on you that you barely know the woman across from you because the only connection the two of you had were the kids. You realize that life just passed you by, and where did it all go?

The Lord showed me something. I started to see that there is one thing in life more important than money, and that is time. Time is so precious, and you can never go back. I know as men, the one thing we would like to have more of is time-because we are always so busy.

I don't know about you, but for me life has gotten much faster, and there is still no extra time. It doesn't matter if you are single or married; we're all still short on time. We need to start making time. For some guys, it may be watching less T.V. For some guys, it may mean less hours at the office. You're right; we all have bills to pay. We think that if we all have thousands of dollars in our account, then that's when we can slow down.

One thing I'm starting to realize is that if you tell yourself, "I'll work Saturdays this year, and next year I'll spend more time with my family," then you just bought into it again. We all know that the more we work, the more we deserve those little extras, and sometimes you find yourself in more debt. There is one thing you can do; start to budget yourself today, and not next year, so you will be able to slow down and spend time with the family.

I can remember thinking of my grandfather (who passed away a few years ago). He had worked hard his entire life in the Forest Industry, and had then owned his own lumber yard for over 30 years. One day he went into surgery, and it wasn't looking very good. As my dad and all of my uncles gathered around him, he had told them; this is what life was all about- family.

He had accepted the Lord and was saved in his late 70's- better late than never. It was nice that this happened 3 or 4 years before he passed away. I had noticed a big difference in him -from how he was before. When I had worked in his lumber yard, let me tell you- it wasn't fun. He was always ticked off at something, so we never had the kind of relationship where you could sit on the porch with lemonade. We did have a chance to sit on the back patio once. We were just talking, and mind you it was about the truck and business, but that was the first time I saw him more as a grandfather, and I was thankful for that time with him.

One thing I like is that my friendship with my dad is closer than perhaps his was with his dad. Years before my grandfather passed away, my dad had made a big effort with the Lord to deal with issues towards my grandfather, and they started to have a very good relationship. One of my personal focuses is to spend time with my boy, Kurtis. The Lord has shown me things for his life that I know will take time, but with God's grace, I know I will remain focused. Staying focused is a challenge at times, because in doing so, you put your own goals aside. What I mean by my goals are toys, a newer Escalade, and newer car audio equipment.

I am realizing that as men, we really try to do something legendary- or leave a legacy behind. Cash is sweet, too, but what are we leaving behind? My dad always said that my grandfather had left his boys one thing, and that was a hard work ethic. That he did. I get more detailed about this in other chapters, because I was starting to look at things differently(ex: having to try to teach Kurtis to live on 40 hours a week to make himself available for God's work and purpose in his life).

I hope this chapter has helped you stop for a minute, reflect, and see… what is that "one thing" you are living for?

Chapter Four

THE BALANCING ACT

In my prayer time, I asked the Lord why we (as men) feel pulled in 10 different directions. The Lord said, "Let's look at that", and that is how this chapter came about. Once again, this may or may not relate to you, but I pray that it may help.

This is an example of a man today-saved or not:

1. JOB

8. PERSONAL TIME WITH GOD AT HOME

2. TO-DO LIST

7. RELIGION
- Church Activities

3. ME TIME / DOWN TIME

6. YOU AS A SON
- Living up to Dad'd expectations

4. HUSBAND
- Fine with wife

5. FATHERHOOD
Spending time with the kids

Now it's easy to see why we seem so busy- and I didn't even get into other reasons (like part-time jobs, or how some guys work on farms). I also didn't touch on bills, and all of that pressure. However, I'm hoping that this may allow you to see things more simply. We'll start right away:

1. JOB

Often times as men- and I definitely put myself in this category- we really take pride in our work. There is nothing wrong with this, as long as we keep it in a proper balance. You may notice that when you meet some men, it's; "Eh, how's it going? My name is Joe!" The next response is, "What? So what do you do for a living, Joe?" Now is this a conversation starter, or is it more than that? For some men it may be a conversation starter, but for others- it's their identity. Only you can honestly answer that.

Looking back years ago (to when I first started working), I really wanted to do my best. I was one of the youngest Semi Owner Operators in Canada. I had just turned 22, and I had a business of my own. Dad helped out by co-signing for me when I got started. I took pride in the fact that I worked long hours to show dispatch and dad that I could do this.

One day, I was standing at the dispatch window. The dispatcher was talking to a guy from another department (refrigerator division). He told him, "If you're ever looking for a good driver, that's the guy you're looking for!" At first, I was insulted- thinking that he wanted to get rid of me! Then it dawned on me; Oh- he wanted me to go back out! I told him I was out of hours, and he laughed. I saw now that he was serious, so I asked him, "How do you know that?" He said, "We go with if you're on time for pick-ups and deliveries, speeding tickets, and customer satisfaction". He told me that I was one of the top 10 drivers in the company (at the time we had about 200 drivers). I felt so proud then, and said, "Are you sure you don't need anything else done?"

That's something that always stuck with me- even though he's working at a different company now. It was just the fact that I was recognized for trying my best. I put a lot of weight into that, and trying to keep it up was challenging at times. Then I started to see that a lot of it was pride. The Lord really began to show me that clearly. Years later, something happened.

That year, we had been scheduled to work 42 Saturdays out of 52. It was a big year, and out of the 42 Saturdays, I worked 40 of them. One Saturday the truck needed to go into the shop, and the other Saturday, we had a chance to go away. Heidi was working 2 part-time jobs in nursing homes, and everything lined up for us to leave for a little weekend getaway.

So...I let dispatch know that I needed the next Saturday off, too. Let me tell you...all hell broke loose! They weren't too happy with me, and I was upset because I felt that they thought I wasn't a hard worker. This time, the Lord showed me that I needed to start getting my priorities in order, so Heidi and I went away for the weekend.

Two weeks later, another company outbid us by a couple of cents per mile, and I lost my run. Just like that, I was at home, and looking for work. Even though we lost the run, it wasn't dispatch getting back at me; the Lord was teaching me that I had to start putting Him and Heidi first. When I sat down, and really looked at it, I realized that I was a number on the wall. That's what I was to them in a nutshell- a number to be replaced at any time.

2. THE TO-DO LIST.

As men, this seems to never end, and really...it doesn't. Please hear me out; I'm not saying to let the house fall apart, but if we look at it; we're always trying to have something on the go. I'm not one of those Handyman guys, but I love seeing the grass freshly cut-nicely and in a straight row, as well as keeping the SUV and car clean. It makes me feel great, but I've also missed getting together for breakfast with men.

I started to see that there were windows of opportunity-and that's exactly what it means; windows that open and close. Quickly. If you start listening to what you are saying, you'll hear yourself.

I would always start a conversation by saying, "Keeping busy?" That phrase could make the person feel lousy if they weren't busy. Some guys would talk for 10 minutes about how busy they were, and some guys would say that they weren't that busy. That's when

I would tell them, "It must be nice to be able to relax". Then I talked about how busy I was. Just a head's up; you may be surprised that perhaps guys won't think of you when it comes to upcoming events or activities. It may become a little joke that starts up; "Don't ask him-he's too busy!"

You may have seen it in the past, or it may even be you. Often times as men, it's in us to take on a "challenge" or a task around the house. What the Lord is interested in is what takes place in the house; the way we treat our wives and our children. You see it once in a while: a nice house, a couple of nice clean cars in the drive way, the grass always cut, the backyard spotless, and the pool always clean.

One day the house is for sale, and you're not sure why? Then you hear that the couple next door is getting a divorce. It doesn't make sense to us as men, because everything looked good. We saw everything from the outside, but things on the inside were a different story. Things on the outside are quick and noticeable (as men we like to get our results quickly), but things on the inside take time and energy. They are less noticeable, but in the long run, they make for a great life!

3. DOWN TIME

Down time for men is very important, but once again- with its proper place. It's easy for it to get out of hand- you look at the long hours at work. I heard on a Canadian news channel once that the average Canadian works 56 hours/week! Our to-do list is on top of that, and that is why we normally see "my time" as right- and deserved!

"Now, it's my time!" We all say this, but "my time" could be anything: golf, football, sporting events, restoring a car, fishing, hockey, etc. It may be easier for you to see it when it's another guy at work talking about working on his hot rod in the garage until 3:00 a.m., or playing baseball all day on Saturday. I will take the liberty to share this with you. Sometimes your hobby may be being involved with something in or for the church.

For myself, it was the men's ministry; studying a lot, and going to men's conferences. That can be the biggest problem, simply because we see it as: "I'm doing the work of the Lord". What we need to understand (as husbands and fathers), is that our first ministry is at home. Please understand me- you really need to pray, and ask the Lord to give you a proper balance. You see it time and time again; people get involved with ministry, and boom! They're gone- with their family left at home. If that's what the Lord wants, then everyone will clearly be on board, and the Lord will give your family the grace. One thing I remember Billy Graham saying was that when his family was younger, he was on the road a lot, and he missed out on them. So this really can happen to anyone.

4. HUSBAND

Normally, it's after everything else is done that we start to take time with our wife. This paragraph will most likely be short, because in another part of the book, I spend more time talking about Communication with your wife. You may be starting to say, "Eh, this relates to me", or "Mind your own business!" I really hope that you are seeing my heart; I do not want to come across as a know- it- all. I can tell you -I have no idea what I'm doing, but I'm trying, and listening to what the Lord asks of me.

5. FATHERHOOD.

I'm going to talk now more from the viewpoint of a son, than from that of a father. The reason that I can share this with you openly is because I have a good relationship with my dad. Dad was always someone I could go and talk to. Mom was also there, but I had more of a connection with dad. Going on truck trips at a very young age, my jobs were: to keep things from falling off of the dash, and to sit on the doghouse (a doghouse was in Cabovers in the late 70's, or early 80's. It would cover the motor, but from inside the truck it looked more like a doghouse).Also, if daddy fell asleep, I was to wake him up slowly. I'm sure the D.O.T. would like that. I always had fun, though, and that's why I became a truck driver. Where else can you be up at 1:00 a.m., having chips on a school night? There was a period (when I was a teenager) that dad went to work- and yes, I was a handful. I can look at it now, and see that dad did a great job.

As a father myself, I can see that mom and dad gave it their all. We lived in a trailer park so that we could go to a Christian School. It's clear how big of a sacrifice that was on their part; we could have lived in a bigger house with a newer vehicle, but they made it a priority.

Dad always loved me- there was no doubt, and he loved my kid sister and my older brother. However, for him to say "I love you" was a bit of a challenge back then. This was due to the way he was brought up. During my father's childhood, he was the oldest, and the one who had the most responsibility and pressure. My grandfather would be gone in the bush for months at a time, so being able to sit, talk and share was tough. When dad gave his life to the Lord at age 31, he now had a new Father, and a new way of looking at things.

I can remember looking for my place in life. I had great friends, with one in particular-Vaughn-that I've had now for 27 years. I was starting to become a man, and I was looking for that approval (or respect if you will). That's where-as fathers (please handle this with care); it is a very difficult time. You remember when you were at that age. I'm thankful that dad started to spend time with me- going out to a truck stop at 10:30 at night just to go out for a burger, or taking me to my first tractor pull at 14. I tell you, guys- that meant so much to me at the time. Dad was not just treating me like a little man, but respecting me as well. Heidi always asked me, "How can you be so confident?" That is something that was instilled in me as a young man.

Without even realizing it, dad was imparting confidence to me, sometimes by just being there. As a typical teenager, it was cool to pretend I wasn't listening, but I heard every word. I didn't see it at the time, but dad was investing time into me.

Once (when I was 21), I was going to look at a car. It was a Wednesday, and dad was going to his meeting at church. I asked him to come with me, and he said, "You know what to look for". So...I went off by myself and looked the car over from top to bottom. I can tell you that there were a couple of screws loose on a panel-yes, I looked at it that closely. I purchased the car, and then I went to the bank. The payments were double that of my last car, and I panicked. I told the woman in the loans department that I needed to make a phone call, and stepped out of her office. I called dad up, and told him the payments were $285.00/ month. Dad laughed, and said, "Don't worry about it; you'll be fine". Just like that, I walked back in and signed the papers. Why? Dad said I was going to be o.k. He showed me that he had confidence in me. I never realized how much I leaned on his encouragement.

A few years later, at a large gathering, I was talking to a young man. He wanted to get a 5L Mustang one day, too. His older brother-in-law laughed, and said, "You're going to need to make more than $7.00/ hour to get that car". Right away, his father said, "Yes, and get your own insurance; I don't want a car like that on my policy". You know what, guys? I saw his head go down, and he said, "Oh well, it was just a thought". I immediately told him, "You can get one. I had one at $7.00/ hour. It can be done". I realized right then and there that my dad had believed in me, and I thanked him later that day. It made a world of difference then and it still does- even to this day. You'll never know how you impact your children. I've been able to learn a great deal from that, and now (with prayer), I'm going to try to be the best father I can be.

I shared this story out of respect for my father. Often as fathers, we think, they'll grow out of it, or, they won't remember that. You'll never know the impact that it may have on your children's, your grandchildren's, or your great- grandchildren's lives. Just spending time with them means more than you'll ever know.

I think of all the men who've worked 6 days/week at the Big 3 automotive plants for the longest time. They may have missed out on their kids' soccer games, birthday parties, or just going out for breakfast with them. These men really gave their lives to their company. One day they got there, and the gates were locked. That was it-they were out of a job. It would be easy to get upset, and to feel taken advantage of. I know we have bills to pay, but the one thing (by the grace of God) that Heidi and I started to change was our spending habits. This way, we wouldn't feel the financial pinch as much. Yes, men…I had to give up upgrading our SUV, getting the Camper, and buying our big bedroom set, but this is a seed we planted together, and I am looking forward to seeing the crop in the future.

6. The PRESSURE of being a SON.
This part may be a bigger or a smaller part for you.

The bigger part example:
Your dad owns a law firm in a big city, and has a big name. You now have a bigger pair of shoes to fill.

The smaller part example:
Your dad works in a factory. You work in an office, and you don't feel much pressure.

I think we all have a little something in us that wants to make our dad proud of us. Seeking their dad's approval (for some guys) has made them who they are today. For others, it explains why they are always mad at their "old man". I was always somewhere in the middle; trying, but not really knowing what for. Dad had a '69 Firebird. At a young age, I wanted very badly to get the rival car- the Mustang Cobra GT. Dad worked hard, and so did I, but I was beginning to see a pattern.

My grandfather worked hard, my dad worked harder, and I guess I would have had to work even harder. I was starting to realize that I couldn't do that and have a life at the same time. It hit me pretty hard, but I never let on. I can remember pulling up with my Semi at a family gathering. I had a show truck with all of the bells and whistles on it. Dad and I added up the cost of the toy, and it came to roughly $60,000.00 of extras. The bumper itself was $6,000.00 U.S. It had come out of Austria, and was made from very thick, pure aluminum. So…I had all of the toys on it, and my dad had helped me big time to polish it up. My grandfather looked at it, and everyone was impressed, but it dawned on me, "Where do I go from here?"

The truck had won the truck show of the year with the previous owner, so I thought, what do I need to do next to keep that up? If you notice, everything about this was in my thoughts. Yes, there are fathers out there who make it more difficult for their kids- so that they can toughen up-but it doesn't make it right. I'm thankful that dad was always there- encouraging me. When I turned my life around (back to the Lord), I started to look at things much differently.

My attitude quickly went from, "I need to have all of the things that I want" to "I want what He wants for me". That was my prayer, and the first thing I noticed was that I needed to spend more time with the Lord. As I did this, things became clearer to me, and I was beginning to ask more questions. One was, "Why was it that when the big 3 automotive plants blew their trumpets, my life went on hold because they needed brakes, door panels and dashboards?" Another was, "Why did Heidi have to make plans by herself on a Saturday?"

At the time, the truck was paid for, and I was asking myself... why? Why push myself so much? Please understand; dad was not a guy who gave me a hard time. However, if we were scheduled to work, and the truck was parked, I would get asked, "Eh, is something wrong with the truck?"

In the past, the company for which my grandfather worked often times had seasonal work (ie: Roofing).

Then, he opened up the lumberyard. It was open 6 days/week. I think that's how it started: the office was open, so you went to look for work- if there was work. Plus, it showed that you were a go-getter. Dad had left that business, and was now into truck driving, and that's not seasonal work- that is all year long. You have to pace yourself; otherwise you'll get burned out quickly.

I can remember going up to Peterborough when I was 22 or 23 (that's where my kid brother-in-law was from). I had major chest pains, and pain in my left arm, so I drove myself to the hospital. Mark and my sister, Jocelyne, came with me, and the Doctors started to run some Heart tests on me. They were asking me if anyone in my family had ever had a heart attack at a young age. That's when I started to freak out. Then the Doctor asked me what I did for a living. When I told him that I was a truck driver, he immediately stopped everything on the spot, and asked me how much sleep I had had that week. I told him, "Approximately 18 hours", and he responded "For the week?" The Doctor told me to go home and get some sleep, and that if I continued on that way, I would burn myself out!

Why was I pushing myself so much? I was trying to prove that I could run with the Big Boys. When I really looked at it, though; I was the only one pushing myself-I had no one else to blame but myself.

It has taken a while. Nothing exciting changes overnight, but I'm going in the right direction. I look at the changes dad made from his father, and I look at what God is doing in my life. I think that one day we may end up with our priorities in order. Don't get me wrong: I'm not trying to make everyone around me look messed up so that I look better. Not at all. Everyone is doing the best that they know how to. What I've had to do is to pray and ask the Lord which decision to go with, and also to lead my family. It's hard to tell your dad that your goal now is to work 40 hours/week, try to make a living, be available for the Lord, and to teach Kurtis that as well. It has to start somewhere.

7. CHURCH ACTIVITIES.

Taking time with God is normally the last thing we do as men. Why? Our way of thinking is that if we go to someone with a problem, it shows weakness. However, if we go to the Lord, something else happens: we draw strength and wisdom. I once heard a man say that God was a "crutch", and that he didn't need a crutch. This guy had a very big alcohol problem.

Let's be honest with ourselves. You reach a point in life where things may fall apart, but know this: God is in control. The enemy will tell you, "You can figure it out. You don't need anyone's advice. You're doing fine-plus, everyone is busy with their own problems". When you belong to a church, there is something that happens. You're not alone anymore- that's why it's called the Body of Christ. It means we're in this together.

Our men's ministry slogan is: "Where we battle as one". That means that when someone is going through a rough time, we need to stand together in prayer. Don't let the enemy fool you into believing that you can do it on your own. You can, but for how long? That's the thing I love about working with men- you're not just working with the men, but with their whole family and marriage all at once. If you want to see true revival, get all of the men you know walking in victory, and watch hell's gates get knocked down. The Bible says that where 2 or more are gathered, He is there.

8. TIME WITH GOD.

All of these things are a true balancing act- they really are, but if they're put in the proper order, you will be amazed at how much simpler it really is. That does not mean that life will be any easier; if anything, you may see that the enemy will target you more.

As you develop a personal relationship with the Lord, you will begin to see His heart in true form. The Lord told me once, "All I ever did on earth was good, but yet everyone sees me negatively". We never notice the Lord doing something nice, but yet when it all falls apart, we start asking, "Why, Lord, why?" This is all truly a test to see where our hearts are.

Even as I write this, Heidi and I are going through a rough patch- not in our marriage, but in the business world. I always said, "Lord, You're in control. I would give it all up for You". Sometimes, I think that God allows things to happen- just to see where our hearts truly are. This is not to hurt us, but to test us.

It's like I always said; "If you have God at your side, you can always bounce back". When you really look at it, it's true. That's where Heidi and I are right now. As I write this book, the price of diesel is out of hand. We went last year from being in the plus $1,000.00/month to now going in the hole $300-400.00/month.

The one thing that we still do is try to give as much of our tithing as we can. Now it is out of our hands, and into His.

The Lord has really been there for me as a man. It's difficult at times, but I heard the Lord say, "What is the end result? When you look at it; you sell everything you have worked for, and start at zero, but you have Me, a loving wife, a great son, and an outstanding church". I got home after work with a smile on my face because that day I had really had my ups and downs. But the Lord was truly there for me! The Bible says, "Do not lean on thine own understanding". I have to tell you that a couple of years ago, this would have put me on medication big time! One thing I can tell you is that man, business will fail you at times, but when you build your house on the Lord, it will surely stand!

At one point, we were looking at selling the house, the truck, the SUV, and the whole ball of wax. The SUV was my pride and joy! For years, it was my status symbol of success. I always just acted like, "Yes, it's an Escalade", and pretended to be humble.

There was a lot of pride under there- let me tell you!

Something happened as I was talking to Heidi about it the other night. I was laughing so hard- I had tears in my eyes! Heidi and I were coming out of a very nice hotel once, and there were 4 or 5 men getting ready to go golfing. They also had an Escalade, and up North there weren't that many of them. So…I looked at them, and I was wearing my big watch (which had cost a couple of hundred dollars).I had all of my rings on.

I was wearing the same style of clothing as they were, with my tan shorts and my black golf shirt. I walked by so confidently, saying, "'Morning, guys", that you would have thought we were vehicle brothers… or something! There was a problem right around the corner. The SUV was in London, ON, getting the stereo installed, so when I turned the corner, I was looking at my other vehicle. It was a '95 four door Sunfire. It was a good little car, but nothing to be that cocky about! I walked fast, and got into the car quickly. I looked up, and 2 of them were looking at me, smiling. I thought, they're not smiling, they're laughing at me! My face was red as I pulled out of the parking lot, looking at my thighs. That is something that I will never forget. It's funny now, but let me tell you- not back then! It was very humbling. As you walk closer to God, that goes away. You even realize that things don't really even matter anymore. Do I still like it? Of course, but it isn't everything to me. As I followed the Lord with all of my heart, something began to happen. I saw that the things of this world don't matter, but the people in the world do. So live your life like Jesus would, and the gap between Heaven and earth will get smaller for a lot of people as you lead by example. If you look at it, Jesus has a history of working with average men…so why not you?

The enemy is always out to make us feel like a nobody. He is right, but through Christ, it's a new game with new rules and the deck is stacked in our favor .Men it's time for us to get back in the game!!!

Chapter Five

STARING DOWN A GIANT

This is an area that is close to my heart. It's simple: we as men all struggle with this area. It normally starts in your teen years. You're a little curious, and sometimes it develops into a major problem. Some men struggle with it more than others, but no matter what, there's still a problem. Some of you reading already know this and may have already paid a big price, but to those that may not know: there is a price. The enemy will never let you see the total until it's too late.

I once heard a story of a young man. He was born and raised in a Christian church, but got caught up in this area. He struggled with solo sex (masturbation) and going to strip clubs. Later, he met a beautiful Christian woman and got married, thinking that this problem would go away. Guys, if this area isn't dealt with before marriage, then it will be a problem in marriage. The enemy changes his tactical plan, and you need to be on guard. It goes from, once I do "it" I won't have problems, to… this is it? This is the only cereal I will have for the rest of my life? Be on alert, gentlemen.

Going back to my story, the young man got married. After that, the problem got worse. He started going to massage parlors and getting the "deluxe" package. Every 3 months, he would get an expensive Call girl. One time, he did not show up for the appointment, and the girl called his house. He had accidentally given her his real name, and his wife got the message that she had left.

Guys, in one week, he lost his beautiful wife and his job. He was a schoolteacher, and the school didn't want this to be a problem later. If a young girl accused him of something inappropriate and the school knew there was a problem, then it would be their problem. He lost his house and his family- not to mention his reputation at church and with his friends. He was now living in a one-bedroom apartment with a buddy and cleaning off tables at a café. I guarantee that if he could have seen the end result, he would have looked for and gotten the help that he needed.

Looking back time and time again in my own life, I was so afraid that I had a major problem in this area. I read a lot of books and went to seminars about this exact area. It seemed like I always got the same thing: Scripture and a couple of stories.

That was great, but I was always looking for a more practical answer; one that dealt with everyday life. I can remember coming out of one seminar in particular. I told the Lord, "There must be a different way- not better, just different!" Once again, I had received a lot of Scripture and a couple of stories, but no steps to get out of it. I can remember the Lord saying, "Well, let's look at this together". I wasn't sure what He meant, but a few months later, things started to happen.

The Lord told me to take notes along the way. I had no idea where this was headed, so I just trusted Him. One day (about a year later) I was at a coffee shop with a man, and I was very open about this area with him. He said, "This would help a lot of men: It's basic, practical, and there are steps which make it easier to walk away from pornography and lust". Then it hit me: this was what the Lord was doing all along: why He had walked me through and had had me take notes on this area.

This is- without a doubt- a very big and very challenging area for all men. It's never really touched on in churches today. It's not something you can talk about on a Sunday morning. When you look at it, you can't tell if there is a problem in churches today or not. It's not as though you can stand in the front of the church and spot the men with the problems.

This is something that we as men have been able to hide for a long time and normally if it gets out it's too late. Make no mistake- it always gets out. Statistics show us that 70% of men in churches today struggle with pornography. I guarantee that you could never tell.

This is one area in the past that I never had much grace for: 50% of Pastors struggle with pornography. My way of thinking was that they should know better. Then something happened a couple of years ago. When the Ted Haggerty story came out, I just rolled my eyes and thought, well, there goes another one! Pastors who were struggling was a hot topic on the Christian radio station and a Pastor had written a book on this subject. As he and the radio host were talking, the Lord really started to convict me. The author was sharing that as men, if our place of employment heard that we were struggling with pornography, not too many of us would lose our jobs.

As a Pastor, it's different. As soon as the problem gets out- if the church cannot afford to keep several Pastors on staff- you're out of a job! You lose your salary, naturally- not to mention the damage on your marriage.

Pastors that struggle in this area are not normally hired back too quickly once the word gets out. These are not excuses, but you can see how they can feel even more cornered in this area.

Also…20% of women struggle with this area. This really struck me! I have never heard women talk about picking up a couple of snacks, pop and porn?! You start to see that we are dealing with a spirit that will go after anyone- male or female. I got all of these statistics at the PK event I attended.

If you really look at it, it always comes out sooner or later. Most of the time, it's by accident, right? You forget the DVD in the machine, leave the magazine out, or just forget to log off properly… and you're busted! I remember talking to a man as we were looking at his new computer. I said, "Well, it must be easy not to struggle with the Internet if you don't have it!" He responded with, "No, we get free Internet at a public place". I asked, "A safe place with all the filters they have up?" He told me that all you had to do was click a couple of things and all of the filters were down. As he was sharing this with me, his eyes got bigger and bigger. Without even realizing it, he had confirmed that this area was a problem for him.

One Scripture that really came alive for me was Philippians 4:13. *"I can do all things through Christ who strengthens me"*.

This is a Scripture for us as men. If you look at the Bible, you see that time and time again we are told to stand our ground; to stand firm. When it comes to lust, the Bible tells us very clearly to run away. If you look at Proverbs 5:8, it tells us to stay away from her doorstep. I am so thankful for this verse, because it shows us that the Lord knew we could not defeat it, so He told us not to go near it. This puts a whole new outlook on it, and gives us hope.

I was once getting ready to speak on this subject with our men at church. I was talking with a good friend of mine. When I told him the topic, his eyes got really big, and he said, "It's all over the place. How do you go up against it?" To be able to "go up against it", you have to be determined to do so. This battle has already been won and given to us. It's because Jesus died on the cross 2,000 years ago that we have victory today.

The Lord told me that to be able to do the right thing in public, you need to start by doing the right thing in private. I wasn't very interested in doing this because no one would see how hard I was trying in private.

If you really look at it though: if you sin in private, the Lord will reveal it, but if you do what's right in private, the Lord will also bring that out.

I need to tell you that I never really struggled with pornography. I think as a teenager I dabbled with it. It started off with a couple of "pictures" hidden in my wallet in grade school. Then in high school, I had a couple of "dirty magazines" in my room. That all stopped one day. I normally hid my magazines in between my stereo towers. As I was installing my surround sound speaker, I moved my stereo to hook it up. Just then, my kid sister walked in the room. I remember it so clearly. I was looking at the wall (at my speaker), and I heard her say, "What is this?" It was still wrapped in plastic, and I knew right away. I had that gut feeling of, Oh my gosh! I didn't want to get thrown out of the house, so I told her to rip it up on the spot and not to tell mom and dad. That stopped that problem quickly.

My strip club life was short-lived also. All this took place in my late teen years. Yes, I was going to church twice on Sundays, and I didn't feel guilty about it at all. I was 16 when I went to my first strip club. I had one of my uncles' ID's. At the time we looked similar, but now I'm about 3" taller and about 150 lbs heavier.

I can remember walking towards the club and being so nervous. When I walked in, I was about 6" taller than the Bouncer. I just raised my chin, like, What's up, man? I let this story out by accident. You see… it always comes out! Dad asked me, "You never got into drinking too much, eh?" I told him, "No, the last time I had a beer my stomach was in knots!" Then I said, "But it could have been the stripper that made me nervous". He laughed. I wasn't laughing, but then I started. It had been close to 10 years. I was then in my mid-twenties, but the last time I had gone to a strip club was when I was 19.

I was very smart back then. I didn't use my car. It was "low on gas", so I took dad's gold Dodge minivan. It had the wood grain on the side- there were about 2 of them in Canada. That color was very rare. What was even more intelligent was that some of dad's buddies from work could have seen it. Someone did see me.

It was a man from church. He asked me if I had been near the area on Friday. The warning lights were already going off in my head. I said, "No, that wasn't me". He said, "Are you sure? This guy had on the same coat that you have". I had a very rare Chicago Bears jacket. It had orange stripes on the arm, and it was official- right from Chicago! I told him once again, "No, that wasn't me!" That put the brakes on for me very quickly.

I started to see that you don't have to go to a strip club, or be on the Internet to struggle in this area. One problem that I really struggled with was lust.

My thought life was my Goliath. The reason that I stayed away from pornography was because you could get caught with it. To me, pornography is something visual: Movies, the Internet, Magazines, T.V., Cable, and even Video Games- which are getting very descriptive.

Lust was my little playground that no one else really knew about. My way of looking at it was that it was my private life. Being in the truck anywhere from 12-14 hours/day, there was a lot of danger in having that much time on my own. In this area, the Lord started with my thought life. I was sitting in church, and there was a young woman-not illegally young. She was standing in front of me wearing a very short mini skirt. I was sitting down, and I just started from her feet... and slowly worked my way up to her head. My thoughts were very, very inappropriate, but at the time I really didn't care. That was a bonus for me, but something happened years later. The Lord was slowly working on my life and heart.

I began to have a new feeling. Conviction. What better time for God to start working on me than when I was doing something wrong?

The reason that I shared this with you, guys, is because -no matter if you're saved or not- as men, this is an area that has impacted us all in one way or another. I was looking in the Bible, and came across Matthew 5:28: *"But I say: anyone who even looks at a woman with lust in his eyes has already committed adultery with her in his heart"*.

My first thought was, oh, He did talk about this. But as men, how do we go up against this GIANT in our land today? The enemy will always make this area in our lives look much bigger than it really is, but as you start to lean on the Lord for your strength, you begin to see the victory on the horizon. You also begin to see that you need to start disciplining yourself. I'll tell you right now: you know when you try to go on a diet, and the Pizza Hut commercials just come alive? Well, hang on...this concept will definitely apply here. The one thing that I can say is that if you take the first step- even though you may feel that you're by yourself- with the second step, I guarantee the Lord will be there. That's why they're called the steps of faith.

Someone asked me the other day if I still struggle in this area. I would have to say, "Yes". But the battles are shorter, and the victories are much quicker. In the past, it would take hours or even days, but now (with God's help) it takes minutes, or even seconds.

As men, I don't think we ever cross the finish line and spike the ball, but we can develop new habits along the way that will help us.

We will get into this topic a little later on. The Steps that we are going to take are very simple, but not easy. I've always noticed (in books and teachings) that they always go from struggling... right to victory! I would always ask myself, "How did they do that?" What were the steps in between? That is what we are going to get into detail about and look at closely- not because it's fun, but because it's needed.

So really... there are 2 parts to this next chapter: the Battleground and staying victorious after the Battle. In the past, I would always try. A couple of weeks later I would say, "This is too difficult!" I would just give in and think, it's everywhere, so why fight it? I would fall

right back into sin. So...we will look at taking ground-
and keeping it!

Gentlemen, let's get ready for battle!

Chapter Six

THE BATTLEGROUND

STEP 1: RECOGNIZE THAT YOU HAVE A PROBLEM.

You need to see that you have a problem. It's not your wife, your pastor or the neighbor. It's you. Say to yourself, enough is enough!

I really want to be set free in this area. Some men may just struggle with T.V. shows or commercials that are suggestive, but they are still stumbling blocks. For others, it may be that they have bigger problems: 2 or 3 hours on the internet, videos, or strip clubs. If you are really looking at getting out of this area, the Lord is there- no matter what level you're on.

The enemy is always out to make it look like you're in control. Then one day you try to stop, and realize that this has a little more pull than you think. It will- and always does- affect your walk with the Lord and your marriage. You can't spend time watching pornography and then go into your "prayer closet" expecting to meet with the Lord. Every time you close your eyes, the images will reappear.

Looking at it simply, you step out from under God's umbrella of protection. You then expect to run back underneath and not struggle. It is not a game to the enemy, and you shouldn't treat it like one. This is just a warning.

As for your marriage: it is pretty easy to see how this will affect the way you look at the woman the Lord has given you. The only time I ever looked at my Escalade and thought it was a piece of junk was when I was looking at a new one. However, when I polished and spent time cleaning it, it was the sharpest car on the road.

STEP 2: CONFESS IT.

James 5:16 *Therefore, confess your sins one to another and pray for each other so that you may be healed. The prayer of a righteous man is powerful and effective.*

I always thought that confessing your sins was a way for God to embarrass you, but it isn't. It's to bring you into freedom. One thing that you must do is to confess it quickly.

The enemy will be very quick to tell you that this is a private matter, and that this is nobody else's business. See this for what it really is: he is trying to keep you from having victory.

If you are looking for an accountability partner in church, you will want to look for a man (whom you respect) who attends church faithfully. You may be tempted to ask the guy who attends church once a month, just so that you can say, "Well, I tried". You must want to be victorious. You will have to find a good friend (whom you can trust) and ask him if he struggles in this area. The reason for doing this is so that you don't just swap stories and create stumbling blocks for each other. Be prepared for backlash. If you're asking someone to help, there are 3 things that you must do:

1. BE HONEST.
2. BE HONEST.
3. BE HONEST.

The reason that I say this is simple. You will be tempted to lie, but you need to be open and really face the challenge. We're all pretty busy men: no one has time to play 20 questions to see if you're being honest or not. Respect his time as well. If it does get out- and it will- that you were lying, then that's a whole new problem. Keep in mind that he is not a priest to whom you can confess, get it off your chest and go right back into it.

The Lord told me once that it was better to be honest about a failure than to lie about a victory.

Begin to pray and ask the Lord for strength.

If you happen to be a man who is asked to be an accountability partner, take this very seriously. You have just been asked to go to battle and to prayerfully stand in the gap for this man. If you're not interested in doing these things, then be upfront about it. Keep in mind that this man may only ask once. He needs someone dependable and trustworthy. Keep it between the two of you.

There is definitely something in it for you. Seeing a fellow brother in the Lord having victory in this area is something that you will never forget. The Lord really put out a challenge for me. He asked me to have Heidi become my accountability partner. Some of you may not think of asking your wife. You may feel that she doesn't understand, but you need to see it from her point of view. Normally when this subject is brought up, she's upset and you're on the defense. This subject is always brought up in a very negative way. If we are real and honest with our wives-perhaps talking over a cup of coffee after the kids have gone to bed- we are setting a completely different atmosphere.

You need to see that there is a spiritual side to it also. When you stood in a church on the day of your wedding, you asked the Lord into your marriage. Now there are the 3 of you in the relationship, so when she prays, the Lord is already there. Your wife can be a powerhouse on your behalf.

She is with you, and wants to see you succeed. However, if you feel that (as a couple) you're not ready, then that is your decision. Perhaps you need to approach a good friend.

I must be honest with you. It was not easy at first. So...I trusted the Lord, and things started to happen. Keep in mind that I never really knew where this was heading, but the opportunity came up. I was ushering at church one Sunday. Heidi was working at the nursing home that day. I always stood at the back of the church to make sure everything was taken care of. A young lady (who has not attended our church for years now) came up and was very friendly. My antennas went up, and little warning lights started flashing in my head. She was very attractive, but she was asking me a lot of questions and talking to me like Heidi would. Slowly taking steps back, and limiting my comments to the bare minimum, I got out of that position. In the natural, I did what was right. Mentally, it was a completely different story.

I started by thinking, maybe she can get her car into the garage. Heidi is at work. Once the garage door is closed, then let the fun begin! My thoughts took off from there. I think the reason that it was even more difficult to stop was because of the flirting. In my thinking, there was a potential of this happening.

On the way home after church I felt terrible. I asked the Lord to forgive me. He said, "Yes, I forgive you, but you need to confess it to Heidi". I really didn't know how Heidi would react. The enemy reminded me of an instance when we were on our honeymoon. Heidi and I were taking a walk, and came across a lingerie store. I stopped and jokingly looked. Heidi said, "I'll tell you right now: if you ever look at a "dirty" magazine, I'll divorce you". I got very upset when I heard that. The enemy was right there, telling me that I had just given her my grapes, and now she was crushing them.

I am thankful to this day. Heidi had put a short leash on me because- in this area- I would have taken any room she would have given me, and ran with it. So…I asked the Lord to give me the strength to honor what Heidi had asked of me. Now with all that said, you can see why I didn't want to share this problem with her. However, I couldn't shake it. Later, I brought Heidi supper at her workplace, and the opportunity came up to talk. I don't have a good poker face, so the first thing Heidi asked me was, "Is everything alright?" I had this image of Heidi shoving her French fries in my face, but I told her what had happened. She was upset- not at me, but at the other girl. I thought, O.k., we're good, but the Lord said, "You're not done".

I confessed my thoughts. Guys, it was like a weight lifted off of my chest! I felt good. When I got home, my thought life was not as difficult because I had euchred myself and my fantasy. I was now able to push away my thoughts because of my obedience to the Lord. He was right there. This leads right into the next step.

STEP 3: THOUGHTS AND FANTASY LIFE.

When the Lord told me, "Men need to work on their fantasy life", I asked Him, "Fantasy life?" He reminded me of the story that I just shared with you in STEP 2. As men, we never really think of ourselves as having fantasy lives. Thinking about it a bit, I realized that we struggle with our thoughts…and they will lead us into fantasies every time. The Lord began to show me: You start by getting a thought. You then have a choice to accept it or to push it out. Using my home church as an example, He said, "If a man came into the glass double doors by himself and our head usher saw a danger, he could deal with it. But let that man go into the foyer. Now you need 2 men. Why? He is further from the door. Let him into the middle of the sanctuary. Now you need 4 or 5 men". You see... the further it goes, the more difficult it is to get it out.

How do you stop your thoughts and control them? There is an act that we struggle with as men. You would never put the two together, but they go hand in hand. Pun intended? That is exactly what we are talking about: solo sex (masturbation). The only way that I can say it is that the enemy is waiting there. As soon as you struggle, he downloads a bunch of images to you (like you would on a GB stick). Another way of looking at it is that you're signing up for one thing and not seeing that the enemy put 10 carbon copies under the first copy. You think you're getting one thing, but you get hit with other problems. There is a very powerful key in this.

In starting to deal with masturbation, the first 3 days were absolutely brutal- I could have literally climbed the walls! It was a very big physical challenge. After that, it was like going past the clouds, out of the storm and into clear blue skies. I saw a big difference in my thought life immediately. Approximately 80% of my lustful thoughts were gone. I was now able to hear the Lord much more clearly. There's a facility in Kentucky that focuses on sex addictions for Christian men. Out of 1,100 men, 67% said that they struggled with pornography. 71% of them said that they struggled with solo sex. It was said that this problem had gone up in the church. What was even more troubling was that it was becoming more of a problem with people in the ministry.

As you can clearly see, men, we are not the only ones. Usually, this topic ends here: with you having the victory. However, the Lord told me that I needed to do more to secure the victory in this area. Now let's look at STAYING VICTORIOUS.

Chapter Seven

STAYING VICTORIOUS

Don't give up any ground.

STEP 4: LOOKING AT YOUR STUMBLING BLOCKS

I am reminded of Godfather III, when Michael says, "Every time I try to get out, they keep pulling me back in". What is it that keeps pulling you back in?

Men, in this area, we are always positioning ourselves either to succeed or to fail. Make no mistake about it. Some areas are:

- T.V. / CABLE / VIDEO GAMES
- MOVIES / T.V. / SIT COMS
- INTERNET / MUSIC

T.V

I've always found myself struggling with lustful thoughts-especially after 9:00 p.m. It seemed like all of the T.V. stations were trying to push the envelope a little bit. You saw stuff late at night, and then you battled all day long the next day.

MOVIES

That one was easy. I would look at the back cover for anything that involved sexual content or nudity. If I found it, I would have a choice to make: look at it, struggle and potentially fall, or ask God to give me strength and put it down. As you obey, He gives you more and more strength each time.

INTERNET

Heidi and I had it for a couple of weeks, compliments of one of our neighbors' wireless network. I came across You-tube-which was awesome! I could type in the name of any of the cars I wanted to see race. At the push of a button it was right there! It was amazing! When a guy at church told me to be careful, I said "Oh, I know. It is very addictive". I was spending 3 to 4 hours a day looking at all the cars and the carshows. After coming across a wet-t-shirt contest, I battled for days. That explained why the guy at church had said to be careful. I didn't know that kind of stuff was on there. I was proud of myself for not looking at it, but just knowing that it was there was very challenging. While praying in the truck, I was very open. I told the Lord that just knowing that it was there waiting for me was now a problem. I was very blessed: the Lord heard my prayers.

Heidi and I were trying to look up campers on the internet one time. We lost the signal for the internet access… and with it went all of the struggling! Just knowing that it wasn't there anymore took all of the pressure off of me.

VIDEO GAMES

I was never a big player, but the images of the girls on the new games are getting very detailed…and very graphic. You have to be very careful now. The enemy will use anything to try to hook you back in.

MUSIC

This was big. Music was my life. I chose not to follow the Lord for years, knowing that He might try to touch this area of my life one day. This was going to be my guilty pleasure- that I didn't want to touch. You may be thinking, music? I know. I never thought that these two areas would ever cross paths, but they did. I loved the 80's hair bands and all of the heavy metal stuff. When they would come out with a love song, it would always be great!

Going down the highway one day, I was talking with the Lord. Out of the blue, I started to struggle with lust. I had no idea why, but the Lord said, "Turn up the radio". It was a slow song from when I was in my early 20's. At the time, I had liked this girl from church. When I heard this song again, it reminded me of her and what I wanted to do with her. It was all right there- with a snap of the finger! I had a choice to make. Believe it or not, I got mad at God for finding a way to get to my music. It had always been there for me.

I can remember getting into my SUV after church one time. I cranked the radio and took a deep breath - just like a smoker would after a long flight. It felt great! However, my taste in music was starting to change- without even my realizing it. It was getting darker and darker: Marilyn Manson, Rob Zombe, Seven Dust, and Nine Inch Nails.

Now here was God - like a school bully- asking me to give it to Him. I didn't want to. All I could hear Him saying was, "Give it to me". I envisioned Him with His arms crossed looking down on me. Then He said, "No, you're not hearing me. Give it to me. I'll take care of it for you". Thinking back, I can remember saying -just like that-"That's it!" God asked, "That's it?" So I said, "Lord, I need you to take care of this for me". I did not have the strength to do it on my own. He then asked me to do something.

Guys, on the way home from church 7 months later, the Lord reminded me of my old problem. I had completely forgotten about it. He had asked me to throw out my CD's. I had listened, and He took care of the rest. He had taken all of that desire away. Just like that. Now understand me: I did replace it with good Christian music. We serve a great and mighty God. This leads us right into the next step.

STEP 5: GETTING RID OF STUMBLING BLOCKS

You will have every excuse to keep whatever it is you struggle with. You have to want victory. The Bible tells us in Matthew 5:29: *"If your right eye causes you to sin, pluck it out. It is better for part of you to be destroyed than for all of you to be cast into hell"*.

I used to think that was pretty dramatic-until I realized it was a metaphor. If you look at it, you can put whatever you battle with into that verse. It will very specifically personalize it for you. At times, I think we really don't see how much we can do without. At first it will be a challenge, just due to the fact that it may be part of a pattern in your life. However, as you begin to obey the Lord more and more, you will start having victory quickly. The Lord has nothing but the very best in mind for you. He may ask you to do something that you're not sure you can do, but He knows your limits.

T.V

As a couple, the biggest challenge for us was to disconnect the last T.V. antenna. I excused it by telling myself that that was just religion. And...after all, I would just be doing it so people would think that I had a lot of self-control. So the Lord said, "Don't tell anyone then". We had already disconnected the antenna in our bedroom the year before. Heidi would fall asleep early, and I would always stay up late, so it was creating one stumbling block after another.

It took a couple of weeks for me to really see that we needed to get rid of it. This is something that the Lord asked me to do. It is a personal thing that He asked of us, but He may not be asking it of you. One evening Heidi and I were watching together, and the Lord told me to pay attention to the T.V. This was strange. I looked, and I saw the similarities -one show after another. On one channel there was a girl pole dancing, on another there were people dancing very provocatively and still another had people stuck on an island with the girls wearing very revealing clothing. I told the Lord that I was sorry. I got up and disconnected the television.

It freed up a lot of time. I had been watching 30 hours/week on average. I had never seemed to have time to finish this book, but I believe that obeying the Lord opened up the floodgates of my thinking. Why do I say this? Because in 4 weeks I was able to practically finish the book (with the Lord's help of course)! I may have mentioned this before, but it is worth repeating. In taking the first step, you may think and feel that you are by yourself, but with the next step know that you are not alone. He will be there.

I guarantee it.

6. DEVELOPING NEW HABITS

As men, there is no way around it: we are creatures of habit. Just look at your local coffee shop. The same men sit in the same corner every day.

You see the same guy walking every day at the same time. Perhaps you have "your" parking spot at work. If you don't think so, watch how you feel when someone takes it. It bugs you just a little.

See that your habits may lead you right back to your stumbling blocks... and catch it. I had one habit- keep in mind that I was going to church but not following the Lord at the time. Before I was married, there was a truck stop right by the bridge. It was a hole in the earth: they had about 4 kinds of pop and 3 kinds of chips. However, those chips were next to a bookshelf just full of dirty magazines. I would "look" at the chips, but I spent most of the time gazing off at the other shelf. I would then dwell on what I'd seen all day long. Now that habit is broken- due to the fact that they tore the place down. If they hadn't, that would have been an area that would have required major attention to deal with.

For some of you, it could be that billboard you pass on your way to work. Maybe it's that little extra-friendly smile with the girl at the coffee shop in the morning. Perhaps it's that television show that you watch weekly, but may struggle with having sexual thoughts afterwards. There's nothing wrong with having habits. If there's a stumbling block in the middle, however, you may find it very challenging.

There's one habit that I never realized I had. I developed a habit of "checking out the ladies". The reason that I looked was because it started when I was very young. It began in my early teen years, and just kept going. One day I realized that I was in my early 30's, and still checking out girls in their late teens.

With the Lord's help, you realize that you have crossed over to being a dirty old man.

Heidi and I were at the mall one day. I happened to notice two elderly men in the food court. They were eating ice cream and talking. Two very attractive young ladies walked by with mini skirts, and they both watched them go by. Afterwards, they looked at each other and started to laugh. I laughed too, thinking that they were two old perverts. The Lord spoke to me and said, "What is the difference between you and them? Sometimes you check out girls in church- even though you are old enough to be their father". I never saw it that way. How do you break a very large habit like that? It takes a lot of discipline and prayer- it really does! If you're going through town, look at the car in front of you. If there's a girl walking along the sidewalk, watch his head. If he is by himself, 99% of the time he will look.

The strategy that I am going to share with you will take you from having a 50/50 chance of making it to a 100% victory. To attain this, there will be one simple-though challenging- task. It's not easy, but it can be done! Being by myself as a truck driver, this was challenging. There was a sign for a gentlemen's club that I always had a problem with. As soon as you enter Canada, there is a very large disgusting sign posted at a major intersection. At the time, I hauled an average of 43,000 lbs/load. Needless to say...I wasn't moving very fast. I always found myself at that light. I would be trying to look forward, but something-like a vacuum-would always be pulling my eyes to the sign.

I would get mad at the fact that I was always failing. I asked the Lord, "What can I do?" He told me to physically turn my head to the left- the exact opposite of the sign. This accomplished 2 things:

1. I was telling my flesh that I was in charge.
2. I was in control of what I was going to let in my vision.

Taking authority over your flesh in the natural also puts you in a wise position spiritually. Something different began to happen each time I came to that light. I would smile and look at the gas station across the street. I knew that I was winning the battle every time, and I was also starting to develop a new habit- without even realizing it.

I had stopped crossing the Bridge for a while. We were once coming back from Florida as a family, and went through that intersection. I was wondering why I was looking at the gas station. The Lord told me, "You have now developed a new habit of looking away". I hadn't even realized that we had gone by the sign. Now I'm working on a new habit in church. Men, that's where it should start . You see it all the time: a hot girl walks in. Look at where all of the other men's eyes go...right to her backside.

Some men are smoother than others. What I try to do is to look at the middle speaker or the pulpit. I know that the next look may be the one that pulls me back in.

The Lord told me something once as I was going down the highway. That's why I always have a pad and pen in the seat next to me now. He said, "Look at a girl wrong and it brings a thought. A thought brings in a fantasy. A fantasy may bring in a physical act. Stop the look, and that will stop the thoughts. Stop the thoughts, and that will stop the fantasy. Stop the fantasy, and that will stop the physical act.

If you look at it, guys, the enemy has attached it all together. For some of you, as you try to do one thing, everything else comes with it.

All I can say is, "Gentlemen, make your next decision the right one. You do this a couple of times in a row, and before you know it, you're on the right track. You will see that the Giant that was in front of you is now under your feet- where he should be (by the grace of God).

Chapter Eight

COMMUNICATION WITH YOUR WIFE

I can remember going to a wedding when I was younger. The bride was exiting the church with her very proud husband. His chest was puffed out, and he was wearing a white Tuxedo. Now you know that it's a few years back. She had tears running down her cheeks, and you could tell that he was holding back- knowing he was now a man. I could see that they were in love- there was no doubt about it. Then, years later, I heard about a very ugly divorce. Even back then, I was thinking, what happened? How did that happen? I was always trying to figure it out, but it wasn't until years later that I began to understand. There was something missing.

That something- believe it or not- is a multi-billion dollar industry today. Communication. We are now able to be contacted anywhere in the world. Home phones, computers, e-mail, text-messages, cell phones, blackberries, pagers …it's all out there. Most of us have at least one of these, and yet the biggest problem we face with our wives as men is communication. Now this is the good part: you get to look at your parents and grandparents, and blame them. Just kidding- but they do play a role. Every relationship is different, and at different levels of communication. I can remember staying at my grandparents' house for a few days. This was years ago. I didn't pay much attention then, but I realized it later on.

My grandfather would come home at 12:00 sharp, and his soup would be on the table. He would sit down, my grandmother would sit as well, and he would talk about work. He'd talk about how the business was good that day. The next day could go badly, but my grandmother was always there to encourage him. That worked for them. They were married for 52 years. My grandmother told my dad, "When you get married, don't even think of coming here. You stay home and deal with your own problems". That's what mom and dad did growing up. It was something! I saw that mom and dad would work through their problems. They would talk, sometimes at a higher dbs level, but they would always get it talked out. I saw this, and began to pray that God would give me a wife who loved to talk (which is dangerous, because I can't shut up).

I do admit that in the beginning of our marriage, I was going to church, but not following the Lord at all. Heidi and I loved to talk, but it was more about personal goals. Paying off the house was a big one. Another topic was car audio. I loved it! It's something I still like today. Then the Lord turned my life around. Believe it or not, that's where the change started. It had been easy to talk, but now I had to share my feelings, and that was very rare. I was never, ever taught to do that- especially with being a 6'3" truck driver. Opening up and sharing was a very big obstacle in itself, but it was something that needed to be hit head-on.

I was so blessed to have the Lord there every step of the way. As I got closer to Him, things that didn't bother me before would now knock the wind out of me. One time, Heidi and I got into a good one- no yelling; just arguing. Heidi said a comment that she had used in the past. I had never cared before, but this time it hit me good! It was nothing major, but I will admit that I was not being nice. Heidi said, "I wish the men at church could see the way you're acting right now". I was involved with the men's ministry. I had a leadership role, and it was something I took very seriously. When Heidi said that, I grabbed my cooler, and headed out the door.

On my way to work, I was not happy. I was very offended, and I can remember thinking, I won't be talking to her anytime soon!

On the way to Flint, MI, I started to pray. I was at the GM plant, so I knew that I would have lots of time at the dock to think. The Lord put it on my heart to call Heidi. First, He asked me to ask her for forgiveness. Then, the Lord told me that both of us needed to make a list of things that we would normally say to each other that hurt us- perhaps not in the past, but now. The biggest one for me was being told that I was not acting the same at home as I was at Church. I didn't want to be a hypocrite. Heidi hadn't realized this had hit me so hard.

There was something "little"- or so I thought- that I would say to Heidi, but she felt that I was attacking her as a new mom. I wasn't, but as we began to share our lists, and with God's help, we began to work on these things as a couple.

That's when I started to realize the difference between "talking", and really talking. Please don't get me wrong; you don't have to go super deep every time you talk. It just helps to know that the door is open if need be. Sometimes, light talk is needed. If it's always heavy, you can also get hopeless. Learning to communicate with your wife is never too late, but it is absolutely necessary to have a successful marriage. Let me tell you; it is hard work, but it does pay off- trust me. One time, years ago –I see it now- the Lord had a divine appointment for me.

I would go and pick up in a small town in Michigan called Homer. I ran there for 2 years. One day there was a new guy that started to pick up for the Chicago area. The first couple of weeks, I gave him the "chin up", and a quick, "How's it going?" Then something happened that was very strange.

My forklift driver was a little late one day, and that never happened. Keith was usually in the trailer before I even backed in the dock. They were very fast (in 15-20 minutes –tops), but one day, Keith and Mike were both in a meeting. The new guy (I never got his name, but he really exists) and I were standing there. We were watching them make brakes as we waited. He just came out and said, "My marriage is in the (and I'm editing this) crapper!"

I didn't know what to do! My first thought was, Lord, I really need your wisdom right now. He could have been a drug user, or an alcoholic! I didn't know if there was a reason why he was struggling in his marriage.

I said, "Lord, I need to know more", and he started to explain.

"This is my 2nd marriage, and my wife's 2nd marriage, and I just don't see it working out". I asked him if his wife knew this. He replied, "We try talking about it, but it always ends up in a fight". I asked if he wouldn't mind telling me what the fights were about? He said that his kids were older and out of the house. He had 3 new stepchildren now: ages 14, 18 and 20. The children weren't showing him any respect, his wife would not back him up on anything, and he felt like giving up.

Now to me this was big. I quickly said, "Please, Lord, I need You", and He was right there! I asked him if he had ever tried to change the environment for this topic. He looked at me, and said, "I have no idea what the hell that means!" I explained that changing the environment was trying something different: not always going back to the living room or kitchen. There always a place in the house where the argument (or the spirit) is waiting for you. Next, I asked him if he trusted the kids at the house by themselves. He said, "Sure, I guess. They won't throw any big parties". I suggested asking his wife to go away overnight, and then taking her out for supper. It didn't have to be expensive, but it would create a positive atmosphere. They could even go and sit by the indoor pool. It was winter, so this would have been very relaxing. I jokingly told him that one night away would be one hour's salary for a Divorce Lawyer, and we both laughed.

After that, he left abruptly. I have to admit; I was scratching my head. His load wasn't even ready. He came back 10 minutes later, telling me that he had just called his wife in the truck. When he'd mentioned it to her, she said she hadn't realized that truckers had feelings... and laughed! He told me that she was excited about the idea; she was already packing! It was Thursday, and he had Friday off.

I wasn't going to ask him about it on Monday, because I thought it would be tacky, but he came up to me. He said they'd had a great time, and had been able to get through a lot of things...and be open. That is a key word. As men, being open has never, ever been a strong point. It's something that's really tough, because we're all learning. Before the Lord turned my life around, I would refer to them as "Oprah moments" or a "tampax commercial". Very nice!

As you can see, the Lord had his work cut out for Him!

One of the biggest misconceptions about men is that we don't have feelings, and that we don't like to talk. For some guys, this is true, but the majority of us need to work at it on a daily basis. I've noticed something about men and men's ministry (with studying and reaching out a lot). There's this idea out there that we have to "toughen" everything up. Crack open the brandy and bring out the cigars! What we need to see is that our relationship with God and our wife is not just a natural thing. An inner spiritual thing takes place. As men, we need to see that.

At first it is different. It's a change and a struggle, but we have our whole lives. This may take time and perseverance, and it's not always easy. However, as you start to talk to your wife more and ask questions, you begin to see more. I heard some guys in the past saying, "My girlfriend is always pissed off!" Ask why. Maybe it's something you can help her with, and if not- put her at the curb and start from scratch. JUST KIDDING! That is a decision you may have to make, but as a married man, there is no curb, and there are no other ships (or fish) in the ocean. This is it- until death do us part. The Lord takes that seriously, and so should we.

These are some of the ideas that Heidi and I had when we were asked to teach a class on Communication Between Spouses. This was really weird, because the first thing I did was glance at the sign-up sheet. Yes, I realized very quickly that we were the youngest married couple in there. When I talked to Pastor Claude (one of our great pastors) about it, he said, "It happens once in a while", and laughed.

So... we went into the room fully armed with a water bottle, sweat towel, and a fan! This is what Heidi and I shared. I hope that these are helpful ideas:

1. NEGATIVE THOUGHTS.

The first thing to watch out for is negative thoughts towards your wife. This is where the true battle begins (ex. He or she did that on purpose!). We've all heard that little voice. That is clearly the enemy. For us as men, we need to try to think of our wives positively... especially at work. That is where we spend the most time thinking- whether positively or negatively. For myself, it's a big challenge to have a lot of free time to think in the truck. However, I also had some of the biggest victories there.

2. TO IDENTIFY YOUR SPOUSE'S LOVE LANGUAGE.

Their actions speak louder than words. My love language is to have Heidi make me fancy meals...I love it! Heidi's love language is for me to take her out on dates (which is still an area that I need to work on).

3. PRAY.

Ask God for His wisdom and what you can do to better the relationship. Often times we ask God to change our spouses, but we should really be asking Him to change us. You watch: your spouse will change.

4. MAKE TIME.

We are all busy-there is no doubt about it! Statistics show us that couples spend less than 4 minutes/day really sharing and being open. It's easy to talk, but sharing is more difficult. Heidi and I enjoy car rides, overnight getaways, and couch dates. It doesn't always have to be expensive.

5. PICK A GOOD TIME.

Heidi and I always try to have worship music on (because it welcomes the right spirit). Pray before. Be careful: if your wife or husband has had a rough day, the conversation may already be headed down the wrong path.

6. KEEP IT POSITIVE.

If you don't, someone is going to get hurt and nothing really gets resolved. I personally had to watch myself. I love to joke around and be sarcastic, but this isn't the time.

7. KEEPING YOUR FOCUS.

Caution: it may turn into a to-do list or about the kids. Stay focused on you as a couple.

FOR WOMEN

This is not an excuse: men have a hard time sharing and showing emotions. How many of you remember seeing guys sharing and opening up on the playground? We just took it on the chin and kept it bottled up. This takes time, effort and work. For most men (not all) 90% of their emotion is anger. I can remember one Wednesday evening. Heidi and I had had a great evening, just relaxing and enjoying each others' company. The next day was our banking day. I went to look at the bills, and saw that things were going to be a bit tight this time. I got frustrated quickly, and I went to bed upset. It just showed me that the statistics were accurate.

Sometimes you may notice that as men we like to switch topics quickly. That is sometimes mistaken as ADD (Attention Deficit Disorder). In reality, if we don't have the answer, we like to move on. Also, another area that begins to change is that as we draw closer to the Lord, we start being more sensitive. Things that didn't bother us before bother us more now, causing offense and hurt.

In the past, Heidi and I made lists of topics or words that would hurt and offend each other. Without realizing it, the things we said really mattered. We each didn't want the other to know that it cut deep. To be honest, we were building a wall of offense between us. As we sat down and really started sharing, we began to communicate.

I recently heard of a new "trend". In this new philosophy, individuals believe that if they take care of themselves first, then they will be better for their spouses. In fact, it is completely the opposite. We should be willing to develop a lifestyle that centers around giving of ourselves. This is the only way that you will ever have a successful marriage. I know that there are many other great books out there that focus much more closely on marriage. I'm just hoping this gets the ball rolling.

Pat Brochu is available for speaking engagements and personal appearances. For more information contact:

Pat Brochu
C/O Advantage Books
P.O. Box 160847
Altamonte Springs, Florida   32716

To purchase additional copies of this book or other books published by Advantage Books call our toll free order number at:
1-888-383-3110 (Book Orders Only)

or visit our bookstore website at:
www.advbookstore.com

or

www.TheBalancingAct.ca

Advantage
BOOKS

Longwood, Florida, USA
"we bring dreams to life"™
www.advbooks.com

Printed in the United States
144327LV00001B/2/P

9 781597 551748